Hey-How for Halloween!

All the witches to be seen,
Some black, some green,
Hey-how for Halloween!
Anon.

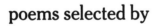

poems selected by
Lee Bennett Hopkins

illustrations by
Janet McCaffery

Harcourt Brace Jovanovich
San Diego   New York   London

Every effort has been made to trace the ownership of all copyrighted material
and to secure the necessary permissions to reprint these selections. In the
event of any question arising as to the use of any material, the editor and
the publisher, while expressing regret for any inadvertent error, will be
happy to make the necessary correction in future printings. Thanks are due
to the following for permission to reprint the copyrighted material listed
below:

CRICKET: THE MAGAZINE FOR CHILDREN for "The House of the Goblin" by Susan Brown from *Cricket, The Magazine for Children*, volume 1
number 2, copyright © 1973 Open Court Publishing Company.

GARRARD PUBLISHING COMPANY for "Eight Witches" by B. J. Lee from
Arithmetic in Verse and Rhyme, selected by Allan D. Jacobs and Leland B.
Jacobs.

HARCOURT BRACE JOVANOVICH, INC., for "hist whist" by E. E. Cummings, Copyright, 1923, 1951, by E. E. Cummings, reprinted from his volume, *Complete Poems 1913-1962*; for "October Magic" by Myra Cohn
Livingston from *Whispers and Other Poems*, © 1958 by Myra Cohn Livingston; for "The House on the Corner" by Myra Cohn Livingston from
Wide Awake and Other Poems, © 1959 by Myra Cohn Livingston; for "Theme
in Yellow" from *Chicago Poems* by Carl Sandburg, copyright, 1916, by Holt,
Rinehart and Winston, Inc., copyright, 1944, by Carl Sandburg.

HARPER & ROW, PUBLISHERS, INC., for "October" by Maurice Sendak
from *Chicken Soup with Rice* by Maurice Sendak, Copyright © 1962 by
Maurice Sendak.

HIGHLIGHTS FOR CHILDREN, INC., for "Ready for Halloween," originally
titled "Song for October," by Aileen Fisher, copyright 1959 by Children's
Activities.

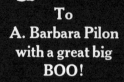

To
A. Barbara Pilon
with a great big
BOO!

OCTOBER

In October
I'll be host
to witches, goblins
and a ghost.
I'll serve them
chicken soup
on toast.
Whoopy once
whoopy twice
whoopy chicken soup
with rice.

Maurice Sendak

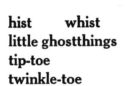

hist   whist
little ghostthings
tip-toe
twinkle-toe

little twitchy
witches and tingling
goblins
hob-a-nob   hob-a-nob

little hoppy happy
toad in tweeds
tweeds
little itchy mousies

with scuttling
eyes   rustle and run   and
hidehidehide
whisk

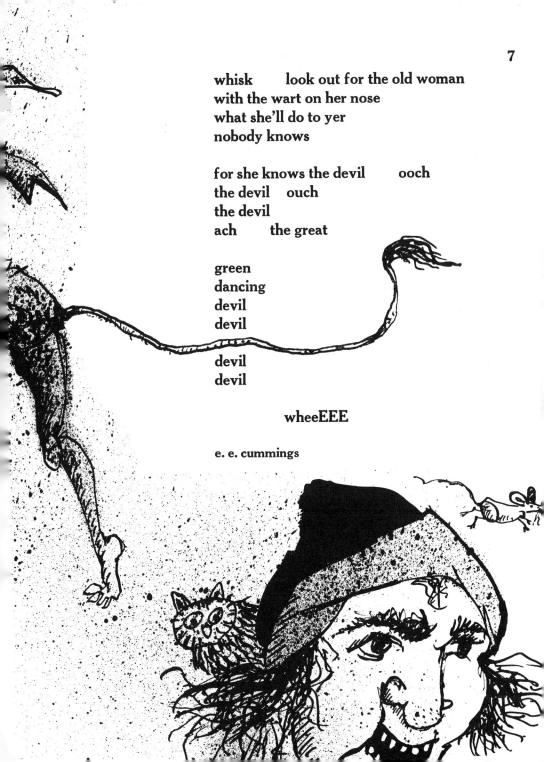

whisk   look out for the old woman
with the wart on her nose
what she'll do to yer
nobody knows

for she knows the devil   ooch
the devil   ouch
the devil
ach   the great

green
dancing
devil
devil

devil
devil

wheeEEE

e. e. cummings

LUCK FOR HALLOWEEN

It was a wise old woman
    Who gave this charm to me.
It works the best on Halloween—
    Or so said she!
"Find a four-leaf clover,
    Wear it in your shoe,
Right foot, left foot,
    Either one will do.
It will lead you into luck
    Before the day is through."

So find a four-leaf clover,
    And put it to the test.
It *might* work anytime—
    But Halloween is best!

May Justus

A RIDDLE: WHAT AM I?

I was the one they chose: "See, he's the
Nicest one," they said.
And they carved me out a face and put a
Candle in my head.
And they set me on a doorstep though the
Night was dark and wild,
And when they lit the candle, *how* I smiled!

Dorothy Aldis

HALLOWEEN

Hooting
  Howling
    Hissing
      Witches,

Riding
  Rasping
    Ragged
      Switches;

Fluttering
  Frightening
    Fearsome
      Bats;

Arching
  Awesome
    Awful
      Cats;

Long
  Lantern-
    Lighted
      Streets;

Tricks!
  Tasty
    Tempting
      Treats!

Phyllis J. Perry

CREEPY

When I go out to trick or treat,
I feel a little fright.
There's lots of goblins on the loose,
And monsters out at night.

Who knows what lurks behind that door,
Or hides around that tree?
So just to play it extra safe,
I take my Dad with me!

Keith Hall, Jr.

READY FOR HALLOWEEN

Pumpkins and all,
big ones and small,
apples and pumpkins
and cornstalks in fall . . .

Corn standing tall,
apples and all,
pumpkins to gather
and set on the wall . . .

Cornstalks to lean,
yellow and green,
bright orange pumpkins
with apples between . . .

Apples between,
shined to a sheen . . .
everything's ready
to greet Halloween!

Aileen Fisher

Everyone is asleep.
There is only the moon
And me.

Seifu-Jo

OCTOBER MAGIC

I know
I saw
   a spooky witch
   out riding on her broom.
I know
I saw
   a goblin thing
   who's laughing in my room.

I think
   perhaps I saw a ghost
   who had a pumpkin face,
   and creepy cats
   and sleepy bats
   are hiding every place.

   It doesn't matter where I look
   There's something to be seen,

   I know it is October
   So I think it's Halloween.

Myra Cohn Livingston

THE HOUSE AT THE CORNER

The house at the corner
is cold gray stone,
where the trees and windows
crack and groan,
so I run past
        fast
        when I'm all alone.

Myra Cohn Livingston

EIGHT WITCHES

Eight witches rode the midnight sky.
One wailed low, and one wailed high,
Another croaked, another sighed
Throughout the eerie midnight ride.

One witch's voice was cackly toned,
Another shrieked, another moaned.
The eighth, much younger than the rest,
Made a scary sound the best—
A scream to make the blood run blue:
Yoooo—
   Yoooo—
      Yoooo—
         Yoooo—

B. J. Lee

IF YOU'VE NEVER

If you've never seen an old witch
Riding through the sky—
Or never felt big bat's wings
Flopping, as they fly—
If you've never touched a white thing
Gliding through the air,
And knew it was a ghost because
You got a dreadful scare—
If you've never heard the night owls,
Crying, "Whoo-whoo-whoo?"
And never jumped at pumpkin eyes
Gleaming out at you—
If all of these exciting things
You've never heard nor seen,
Why then—you've missed a lot of fun,
Because—that's HALLOWE'EN!

Elsie M. Fowler

TRICK OR TREAT

Trick or treat, trick or treat.
We Halloweeners roam the street,
Scaring old ladies with our false faces.
We poke out big sacks and pillowcases.
And if people refuse to open the door,
Or give us an apple or nothing much more;
We soap their windows
And soap their doors.
So bring out your dainties
And all things sweet
For this is the night of
Trick or Treat.

Carson McCullers

HALLOWE'EN

Leaf piles smoke in the whispering dark,
Goblins prowl the streets;
Silent witches haunt the park,
Ghosts unfurl their sheets.

Noiseless footfall on the stair,
Thumping in the hall;
Someone knows just who to scare—
And *I* scare best of all!

Barbara Juster Esbensen

THE WITCH'S SONG

Hey! Cackle! Hey!
Let's have fun today.
　　All shoelaces will have knots.
　　No knots will untie.
　　Every glass of milk will spill.
　　Nothing wet will dry.
　　Every pencil point will break.
　　And everywhere in town
　　Peanut-buttered bread will drop
　　Upside down!
Hey! Hey! Hey!
Have a pleasant day!

Lilian Moore

ON HALLOWEEN

The witches fly
Across the sky.
The owls go "Who? Who? Who?"
The black cats yowl
And the green ghosts howl,
"Scary Halloween to you!"

Nina Willis Walter

CAT

The black cat yawns,
Opens her jaws,
Stretches her legs,
And shows her claws.

Then she gets up
And stands on four
Long stiff legs
And yawns some more.

She shows her sharp teeth,
She stretches her lip,
Her slice of a tongue
Turns up at the tip.

Lifting herself
On her delicate toes,
She arches her back
As high as it goes.

She lets herself down
With particular care,
And pads away
With her tail in the air.

Mary Britton Miller

THE HOUSE OF THE GOBLIN

Shouts and squeaks
And terrorized shrieks
   Come from the house
     of the goblin.

Sighs and moans
And horrified tones
   Come from the house
     of the goblin.

The baying of hounds
And sinister sounds
   Come from the house
     of the goblin.

A terrified groan
And then a last moan—
   All is quiet.

Susan Brown

THEME IN YELLOW

I spot the hills
With yellow balls in autumn.
I light the prairie cornfields
Orange and tawny gold clusters
And I am called pumpkins.
On the last of October
When dusk is fallen
Children join hands
And circle round me
Singing ghost songs
And love to the harvest moon;
I am a jack-o'-lantern
With terrible teeth
And the children know
I am fooling.

Carl Sandburg

THREE GHOSTESSES

Three little ghostesses,
Sitting on postesses,
Eating buttered toastesses,
Greasing their fistesses,
Up to their wristesses,
Oh, what beastesses
To make such feastesses!

Anonymous

WHAT WITCHES DO

The witches don their pointed hats,
The witches croak and croon,
The witches ride their broomsticks
Away beyond the moon.

The witches don their flowing cloaks,
The witches stir their brew,
The witches chant their magic spells
All the dark hours through.

The witches stroke their big black cats,
They comb their locks of gray,
Yet when the first faint daylight comes,
The witches hide away.

Leland B. Jacobs

WHAT NIGHT WOULD IT BE?

If the moon shines
On the black pines
And an owl flies
And a ghost cries
And the hairs rise
On the back
    on the back
        on the back of your neck—

If you look quick
At the moon-slick
On the black air
And what goes there
Rides a broom-stick
And if things pick
At the back
    at the back
        at the back of your neck—

Would you know then
By the small men
With the lit grins
And with no chins,
By the owl's *hoo*,
And the ghost's *boo*,
By the Tom Cat,
And the Black Bat,
On the night air,
And the thing there,
By the thing,
    by the thing,
        by the dark thing there

(Yes, you do,
 yes, you do
  know the thing I mean)

That it's now,
 that it's now,
  that it's—Halloween!

John Ciardi

INDEX